ZENDAYA

A Little Golden Book® Biography

By Lauren Clauss
Illustrated by Alyah Holmes

🌹 A GOLDEN BOOK • NEW YORK

Text copyright © 2024 by Lauren Clauss
Cover art and interior illustrations copyright © 2024 by Alyah Holmes
All rights reserved. Published in the United States by Golden Books, an imprint of
Random House Children's Books, a division of Penguin Random House LLC, 1745 Broadway,
New York, NY 10019. Golden Books, A Golden Book, A Little Golden Book, the G colophon,
and the distinctive gold spine are registered trademarks of Penguin Random House LLC.
rhcbooks.com
Educators and librarians, for a variety of teaching tools, visit us at RHTeachersLibrarians.com
Library of Congress Control Number: 2023951459
ISBN 978-0-593-71150-7 (trade) — ISBN 978-0-593-71151-4 (ebook)
Printed in the United States of America
10 9 8 7 6 5 4 3 2 1

Zendaya Maree Stoermer Coleman was born on September 1, 1996, in Oakland, California. Her first name is of African origin. In Shona, a language spoken in Zimbabwe, it means "to give thanks."

Zendaya grew up in a loving home. Her parents, Claire and Kazembe, were both teachers. They taught Zendaya the importance of education.

Zendaya has five half brothers and sisters, and many nieces and nephews. One of her nieces, whose nickname is Zink, is actually a year *older* than she is! Since most of her siblings are much older, Zendaya spent a lot of time with Zink growing up. They are still close friends.

During the summers, Zendaya's mom worked at a local community theater. Zendaya would help out by seating guests and selling raffle tickets. It was here that she discovered her love of acting.

Zendaya was a shy kid, but she knew that she wanted to be on stage like the actors she watched every summer. When she was eight years old, she began taking acting and dancing lessons. Soon she was performing in the theater's productions.

Her big break came in 2009 when she was fourteen years old. Zendaya played the role of Rocky Blue in Disney Channel's *Shake It Up*. The show was about two friends working toward their dream of becoming professional dancers. Zendaya and her dad moved to Los Angeles, and she began her career as a TV star!

In addition to acting and dancing, Zendaya was also interested in singing! She released her first single, "Swag It Out," when she was fifteen. Her self-titled album came out in 2013.

Thanks to her hip-hop and hula lessons as a child, Zendaya had some great moves to show off in her music videos. Her dancing was so impressive she was asked to appear on *Dancing with the Stars*. She was one of the youngest contestants to ever compete on the show—and she came in second place!

Meanwhile, Zendaya continued acting. After *Shake It Up* ended, she starred in the Disney Channel TV movies *Frenemies* and *Zapped* before landing the lead role in *K.C. Undercover*.

When that show ended, Zendaya decided it was time to move on from Disney and start a new phase in her life and career.

"The end of an era," she wrote in a message to her fans on social media. "On to the next. Thank you for continuing to grow with me."

Soon, Zendaya was on movie screens, starring in two of the biggest blockbusters of 2017! From helping to save New York City in *Spider-Man: Homecoming* to performing amazing circus stunts in *The Greatest Showman*, Zendaya showed the world what a talented adult actor she was.

Zendaya also stars in a TV show called *Euphoria*. Her performance was so good she won *two* Emmy Awards for Outstanding Lead Actress in a Drama Series. Zendaya was the youngest person ever to win that award!

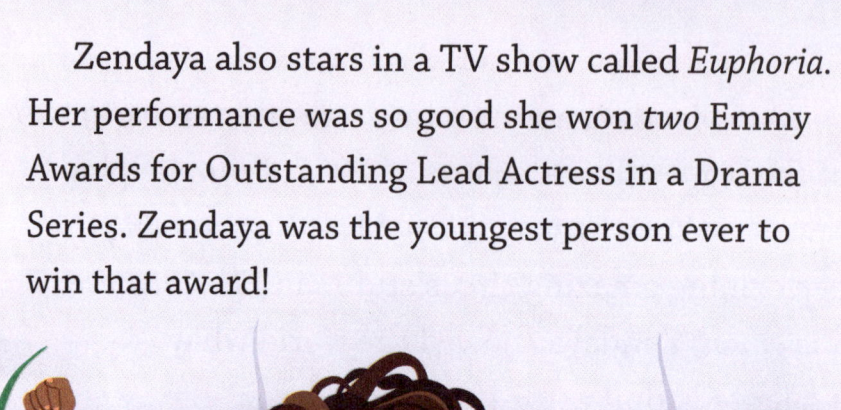

Her first win was in 2020 during the COVID-19 pandemic. Because it was unsafe to gather in large groups at that time, she accepted her award at home, surrounded by her family. It was a very special moment for her.

In addition to being a performer, Zendaya is a
fashion icon. She has modeled for multiple fashion
brands, walked the runway at New York and Paris
Fashion Weeks, and won many best dressed awards.

Zendaya is passionate not just about fashion but about promoting diversity and inclusion in the fashion industry by celebrating women of color and plus size models. Her clothing line, Daya by Zendaya, included clothes for all sizes and genders.

If she hadn't become an actor, Zendaya would have liked to have been a teacher. One way she honors this passion is by working with the #WeNeedMore initiative to provide access to technology and learning for all children.

Through this program, she brought new laptops to the elementary school her mom taught at for twenty years.

Zendaya is a well-known activist, and like her love of acting and singing, this passion started young, too. When she was just six years old, Zendaya and her friends petitioned their school principal to let them perform a Black History Month play. Zendaya portrayed Bessie Coleman, the first female African American pilot.

Since then, Zendaya has used her fame to promote causes she cares about. She's a vocal supporter of the Black Lives Matter movement and an advocate for women's rights and voting rights, often encouraging her fans to vote during election years.

Zendaya is a true star—and not just because of her many movies, shows, and songs. She uses her fame to inspire others to love themselves and work to make the world a better place. Looking at all she has achieved at her young age, who knows what amazing things she will do next!

"You have to have a purpose, and mine is to connect with the world, to get across messages that are important."